ELDER ABUSE, NEGLECT, AND MALTREATMENT

What Can Be Done to Stop It

by

Mary Hird

DORRANCE PUBLISHING CO., INC.

PITTSBURGH, PENNSYLVANIA 15222

ISBN # 0-8059-6235-2
Printed in the United States of America

First Printing

For information or to order additional books, please write:
Dorrance Publishing Co., Inc.
701 Smithfield Street
Third Floor
Pittsburgh, Pennsylvania 15222-3906
U.S.A. 1-800-788-7654
Or Visit our web site and on-line catalog at www.dorrancepublishing.com

To my husband, Sylvester, my daughter, Claudia, and my son, York, for their constant encouragement and steadfast support.

Thank you,
Mary Hird

CONTENTS

ABSTRACT

The researcher investigated the problem of elderly abuse, neglect, and maltreatment. A questionnaire was distributed to thirty participants who were employees of a long-term care center. This center contained five units of which two were rehabilitation units, two were long-term care units, and one was a dementia unit.

The questionnaire consisted of ten questions and each required a response of either yes, no, or undecided. The participants were given one week to respond. Of the thirty questionnaires that were distributed, twenty-three were returned. The responses to the questions were then analyzed.

The study, though limited by the number of responses, supports the concept that elder abuse, neglect, and maltreatment in elder care facilities and communities hinges on the attitudes of caregivers. Greater awareness and reshaping of the attitudes of caregivers towards the elderly could help to prevent abuse, neglect, and maltreatment. Finally, the incidences of elderly abuse, neglect, and maltreatment are increasing.

Chapter One

Introduction

PROBLEM STATEMENT

From time to time several writers and researchers have undertaken to explore and expose certain conditions that are contrary to the well-being of human beings and to their existence. For example: Joe Claderone and Tom Zambito, writers for the *New York Daily News*, have been very persistent in their efforts to investigate and expose conditions of abuse, neglect, and maltreatment of the elderly in nursing homes in New York State. Although abuse of the elderly in the domestic setting can also be appalling, it is felt by this researcher, that elder care institutions should be the places for compassionate care. As one observes the graying of the U.S. population, the increasing life span, and the increase in the number and proportion of elderly in the society, the following demographic considerations must be kept in focus, if the problem of elderly abuse, neglect, and malnutrition are to be adequately addressed:

1. The aging of the postwar baby boom generation.
2. Emigration of other elderly from other countries around the world.
3. Cultural differences in the perceptions of what constitutes elderly abuse, neglect, and maltreatment.
4. Differences in the conformity to reporting standards in the USA.
5. Defects in education regarding elderly abuse both on the community and the elderly institutional levels.

It is estimated that 13 percent of the US population, over thirty-five million, were over age sixty at the beginning of the millennium.

The incidence of elder abuse, neglect, and maltreatment is a major concern that requires both public and government involvement.

Despite all the new reporting mechanisms, it is believed that elderly abuse is still largely under-reported. The exact national incidence is not known, despite various studies but it is hypothesized:

1

   i. that elder abuse, neglect, and maltreatment is increasing.
  ii. that the attitudes of caregivers have a large impact on the increase.
 iii. that health practitioners do not report cases of elderly abuse as the laws require. The main questions that are to be addressed in this study are:
- a) Is the problem of elder abuse, neglect, and maltreatment increasing?
- b) What effect do negative attitudes of health caregivers have on elder care?
- c) Do health caregivers report all incidents of elderly abuse as required of them both legally and ethically?

THE PURPOSE OF THE STUDY

The purpose of the study is to examine the problem of elder abuse, neglect, and maltreatment. It is intended to find answers:

1. That could possibly link the effects of caregivers' attitudes on elder care.
2. To evaluate the reporting of incidents of elder abuse.
3. To find out who are the likely victims.
4. Who are the abusers.
5. What can possibly be done to prevent the problem?

THE RATIONALE OF THE STUDY

It is of growing concern that a large proportion of the society is considered to be senior citizens. As mentioned before, this group is expected to increase. Working in an elderly care facility with several incidents of proven abuse and suspected abuse to investigate, some questions become clear.

1. What is the effect of the attitudes of caregivers on the elderly that they care for? (It is known that sometimes actions are influenced by attitudes).
2. What can be done to change the negative attitudes of caregivers?
3. What can be done to improve reporting?
4. Is the problem increasing or decreasing?

THE SCOPE OF THE STUDY

The scope of the study involves data gathered from newspaper articles, textbooks, and other writings on the topic of elder abuse, neglect, and maltreatment. The main instruments involved in the study are the literature, which will be reviewed in Chapter Two, and a questionnaire developed from participant observation, which will be discussed under the methodology in Chapter Three.

The data analysis and findings of the study will be discussed in Chapter Four and the summary of the study, discussion, and recommendations will be presented in Chapter Five. Included also is a bibliography of the relevant literature used in the study. The appendices are also included.

IMPORTANCE OF STUDY

The study is important because it is designed to examine the attitudes of caregivers to the elderly. It explores who are the likely victims for abuse and seeks to answer the question "Are elder abuse, neglect, and maltreatment increasing?" It will also examine reporting mechanisms, and why family members and other care givers in the domestic setting abuse the elderly. Another point of importance is the response of government officials to some of the abuse outcry involved in the literature. For example some corrective actions projected by government officials are;

- Unannounced inspections of elder care facilities by state inspectors.
- Hiring more state inspectors.
- Setting a par level ratio of care givers to patients in elder care institutions.
- Allotment of more money for care and protection of the elderly.
- Plans to force nursing home owners to hire more staff.
- Better screening and education for staff in elder care institutions.

The study is important as it also gives the opportunity to look at elderly abuse and some of the preventive and corrective measures used in other countries. Elderly abuse, neglect, and maltreatment have a direct, adverse impact on the U.S. healthcare system.

OVERVIEW OF CHAPTER ONE

The chapter focuses on providing an introduction to the study. This involves the reason for researching the topic, the importance of the study, the scope of the study, the rationale of the study, and definition of terms used throughout the study. All of the subheadings relate to the study of the topic of Elderly Abuse, Neglect, and Maltreatment. The research involved will seek to find solutions or answers to the questions:

A) What constitutes elderly abuse and maltreatment?
B) Who are the victims?
C) Who are the abusers?
D) Where are the likely places of abuse?
E) How can elderly abuse be reported? Statistics on reporting.
F) What can be done to prevent elderly abuse, neglect, and maltreatment?
G) What are some of the future predictions on elderly abuse?

From the questions, the researcher directs the research towards the solution of the problem. The provisional conjectures in guiding the investigation are the following:

1) There is an increasing incidence of elderly abuse, neglect, and maltreatment.
2) The negative attitudes of some caregivers may be largely responsible for the abuse.
3) Elderly abuse, neglect, and maltreatment are under-reported by health care practitioners, both in this and other developed countries of the world.

DEFINITION OF TERMS
The following are definitions of terms that will be used throughout the study.

Abuse
According to Webster's Collegiate Dictionary, abuse means:
a) Corrupt practice or custom.
b) Improper treatment.
c) To use so as to injure or damage.

Abuse can involve any or all of the following types;
- Physical Abuse.
- Sexual Abuse.
- Emotional or Psychological Abuse.
- Financial or Material Exploitation.

Abuse can take place both in a domestic setting or in any elderly care institution.

Physical Abuse
The use of physical force which may result in bodily injury, physical pain, or impairment as per (http://www.elderabusecenter.org/basic/html). Physical abuse may include but is not limited to acts such as hitting, striking, beating, kicking, punching, shaking, burning, grabbing an arm or ear twisting, or hair pulling. Physical abuse also includes the inappropriate use of drugs and physical punishment that involves assault and battery. This type of abuse could be intentional or by allowing someone else to inflict the abuse that causes bodily injury, physical pain, or impairment.

Signs and Symptoms
Signs and symptoms include bruises, black eyes, rope marks, skin tears, welts, bone fractures, skin discolorations, swellings, pain or drowsiness, open wounds, cuts, punctures, untreated injuries, bleeding, broken eye glasses, and other signs of punishment or signs of restraint.

Suspicion is also drawn if there is sudden change of behavior or medication overdose or under dose as evidenced by drowsiness or agitation seizures or other medication related disorders.

Sexual Abuse
This is defined by the National Center for Elder Abuse as the non-consensual contact with an elderly person. Sexual abuse includes any or all of the following; unwanted touching, rape, nudity, and photographs of genital or sexual parts without consent of the elderly person.

Signs and Symptoms
- Venereal diseases or genital infections that cannot be explained.
- Vaginal or genital bleeding or lacerations that cannot be explained.
- Cuts and bruises around the breasts and genital areas.
- Stained, dirty, or bloody underwear.
- Pain in the genital area.
- Report of rape, sodomy, or other forms of sexual assault.

Psychological or Emotional Abuse
Psychological or Emotional Abuse is defined by the National Center on Elder Abuse as "the infliction of pain, anguish, or any distress through verbal or non verbal acts against the elderly person. This may include but is not limited to harassment, threats, intimidation, verbal assaults, insults, humiliation, failure to respond to the elderly person, yelling, isolation or locking away, or denigration."

This form of abuse can sometimes be even more painful than physical abuse. It affects the psychological well being of the victim and manifests itself in the victim's behavior. The elderly victims of this type of abuse are usually tearful, fearful, and depressed, sometimes with hands on their cheeks or other signs of depression.

Signs and Symptoms of Psychological/Emotional Abuse
- Withdrawal, non communication.
- Signs of agitation or emotional upset.
- Dementia—like behavior that may include sucking, rocking, or rubbing of body parts.
- Complaints from elderly persons of actual verbal or emotional abuse or mistreatment.

Signs and Symptoms of Psychological/Emotional Abuse
- Unauthorized withdrawal of money at banks or ATM machines.
- Sudden changes in the elderly person's will or other advanced directives.

- Inclusion of additional names on the elderly person's bank card or will.
- Unexplained disappearance of valuables.
- Actual disappearance of an elderly person.

American Association of Retired Persons (AARP) This is an interest group of elderly persons that is regarded as a solidarity group. It is based in part on feelings of a common identity of age, in this case older Americans. (http://www.aarp.org)

Antihyperintensive Medication
Definition: Medication that is taken for the control of high blood pressure or hypertension.

Baby-Boom Generation
Definition: The researcher asserts that this is a term given to people who were born shortly after the end of World War II. These people are also referred to as the Post War Baby-Boomers. These people were born during the decade of the 1940s. This group is expected to greatly increase the elderly population of this and other countries. Government authorities are concerned about the financial impact of this new group of elderlies on the economy and on healthcare. In view of the present proportion of elderly abuse, neglect, and mistreatment, steps are being taken to curtail this problem with the Baby-Boomers who are now entering the senior citizens age group.

Chemical Restraint
Definition: The researcher asserts that this term refers to the situation where drugs or other chemicals are used to subdue, confine, or control the activity and behavior of individuals. This includes the misuse of psychotropic drugs, other illicit drugs, or alcohol. Patients with dementia are the likely ones to be victims of this type of abuse, especially if they are confused. This form of restraint is used both in institutions and in homes. This is different from the use of medications to prevent a patient from injuring him or herself or others to correct agitation.

Physical Restraint
Definition: The researcher asserts that this is the use of certain devices to restrict, or control, or limit the voluntary movement of a person. These are not intended to be removed by the person to whom they are applied. These devices include ropes, mittens, safety belts, bed rails, geriatric chairs, wrist restraints, and vest restraints (used to tie the patient in a position.)

Domestic Elder Abuse

Frances Merchant Carp, in the book *Elder Abuse in the Family*, defines this as a case in which "transactions between persons and environment produce adaptive/maladaptive behaviors and experiences." Here, abuse is a maladaptive outcome.

Domestic elder abuse is manifested in the following ways, including but not limited to physical attack, threatening or intimidating, physical or verbal abusive behavior, unnecessary or demeaning confinement or isolation from others, failure to follow physicians' orders regarding medication and other care, exploitation of the elderly persons' finances, or a combination of these examples.

Elderly Abuser

Definition: The researcher asserts that this is anyone who abuses an elderly person.

Components of the Abuser

A common trait of those who abuse elders to serve their own needs is an underlying poor mental health and psychopathic personality. In other words, many of those who abuse the elderly could have pre-existing psychological problems.

Emphysema

Definition: As per Webster's Collegiate Dictionary, it is a condition characterized by air filled expansions of body tissues; a condition of the lung marked by distention and frequently complicated by impairment of heart action.

Exploratory Laparotomy

Definition: The researcher asserts that this is a surgical opening of the abdominal cavity to explore for answers to an abdominal problem that cannot be diagnosed otherwise.

Financial and Material Exploitation

This form of abuse falls under psychological and emotional abuse. It is defined as the misappropriation of an elderly person's property, money, or other assets. Examples of this type of abuse involve;

- Cashing or using an elderly person's checks without that person's consent, knowledge, or authorization.
- Forging of signature.
- Misusing or stealing an older person's money, jewelry, or other personal possessions.
- Coercing or forcing or deceiving an older person into signing documents such as bank withdrawals, wills, power of attorney, guardianship, or other contracts.

Hypoglycemia
Definition: As per Webster's Collegiate Dictionary, this is an abnormal decrease of sugar in the blood.

Hypothyroidism
Definition: As per Webster's Collegiate Dictionary, a deficient activity of the thyroid gland with resultant lower metabolic rate and general loss of vigor.

JAGS: Journal of the American Geriatric Society.

Living Will
Definition: It is a legal document in which an individual expresses his or her wishes regarding health care in advance in case of incapacitation in the future. The living will should be signed and dated by two witnesses who are not beneficiaries or relatives of the individual.

Neglect
Neglect as asserted by the researcher is the failure or refusal to fulfill any part of a caregiver or relative's duty to an elderly person. This also includes failure to pay for or provide services for an elderly person, whether in the home or institution. This might take the form of failure to provide food, water, shelter, clothing grooming, safety, personal hygiene, medication, or other necessities of life.

Self-Neglect
This is when certain negative behaviors of an elderly person adversely affect their own health and safety. For example; failure to practice personal hygiene, smoking, drug and alcohol abuse, failure to eat nutritious foods, poor financial management. These behaviors are only regarded as self-neglect if the elderly person is cognitive of negative and positive behaviors.

Signs and Symptoms of Neglect
- Loss of weight.
- Unkept appearance.
- Body odor.
- Unclean, unsanitary living conditions.
- Evidence of pest infestation e.g. lice, fleas, mice, etc.
- Poor dental care.
- Foul-smelling conditions.
- Unsafe living conditions: e.g. too cold or too hot, no running water, poor electrical wiring in house, stairs to climb or descend without assistance.
- Poor attention to health problems, such as failure to follow doctors' advice, failure to keep doctors' appointments.

Older Americans Act. (OAA)

P:I 89-73 Established 1965

Definition: This is a federally funded program for older Americans. It involves several programs to assist the elderly. The following are the programs that fall under the OAA:

- Senior Citizens Centers
- Meals on Wheels
- Legal Assistance Services
- Ombudsman Affirmation
- Employment Services
- Family Caregiver Support Program This program provides the following:
  1. Nutrition
  2. Employment training
  3. Community Service Opportunities
  4. Protection against elderly abuse
  5. Assistance and support for families providing services to their elderly

The new legislation (HR782) which President Clinton signed on November 13, 2000, creates a new National Family Caregiver Program and authorizes $125 million for funding. The money will be distributed to provide caregiving training, counseling, respite care, peer support, and other types of assistance. The services will also be available to younger persons caring for younger disabled relatives.

The act established an Administration on Aging to administer programs for the elderly through state agencies on aging. The agenda for the joint efforts of the federal agency and the state agencies was detailed in ten specific objectives for the nation's older citizens, including several that were related to their health, as defined by Beaufort B. Longest, Jr. in *Health Policy Making in The United States 1998*.

Osteoporosis:

The researcher asserts that this is a thinning and weakening of the bones in women due to estrogen withdrawal and reduced calcium to the bones. This causes bones to become brittle and break easily.

Participant Observation

According to *Sociology* by Donald Light Jr., and Suzanne Keller: the definition of participant observation is "A method in which researchers join and participate in groups they plan to study, in an effort to gain first hand knowledge of a way of life." In the case of this study the involvement was to evaluate opinions and attitudes of care givers towards the elderly, also to test the hypotheses that:

a) Elder abuse, neglect, and malnutrition are increasing.
b) Negative attitudes of caregivers result in abuse.
c) Elder abuse, neglect, and maltreatment are under-reported by health care practitioners.

The participant observer in this study is involved with daily operations of an elder care facility. One of the functions of the participant observer is involvement into investigations of reported or suspected cases of abuse of the elderly by caregivers in the long term care facility where the questionnaire was utilized.

Peritonitis
The researcher asserts that this is an infection or inflammation of the peritoneal membrane that lines the abdominal cavity and the pelvic viscera.

Psychotropic Medication
Definition: These are drugs that are used to treat psychiatric conditions. Overuse can be regarded as chemical restraint, as the researcher asserts.

Vulnerable Adult
This was defined by M. Robin Morris in the August, 1998 issue of *RN Magazine*, as a person with a physical or mental condition—such as Alzheimer's disease or an infirmity relating to aging that substantially impairs his or her ability to care for himself or herself. Some statutes cover adults over sixty years of age, according to the article.

Will
Definition: The researcher asserts that, "It is a legal document in which an individual state his or her wishes regarding money, property or estate, children, even burial after death.

"An executor or executors are usually appointed to ensure that the individual's wishes are carried out as set forth in the will."

Summary of Chapter One
The chapter began with an abstract of the study. The following were discussed:

An overview of the study

Problem statement: The overall problem of elder abuse, neglect, and maltreatment: taking into consideration international, demographic, cultural, and ethnic relationships to the problem.

The purpose of the study

The rationale of the study

The scope of the study

The importance of the study

The chapter ended with definitions of terms that are used throughout the study.

Conclusion

The literature review provides positive answers to the three basic concerns listed. Overall, the study revealed that the incidence of elder abuse, neglect, and maltreatment is a major health care problem in this and many other countries of the world. As the baby-boom generation becomes gray, more elderly people will be in the society. Many elders are projected to be institutionalized, while others will receive care at home. It has been proven that a large proportion of elderly abuse takes place both in homes and in institutions. Despite all the new reporting mechanisms, elder abuse is still considered to be largely underreported. The exact national incidence is not known, despite various reports, most of which are estimates. For example, in 1991 researchers estimated that 2.5 million older Americans were victims of different forms of abuse, neglect, and maltreatment.

Some of the risk factors identified are chronic diseases leading to poor health, cognitive and/or physical impairment, alcohol and drug abuse, poverty, and domestic violence.

Several writers have written on the topic. Recently several newspaper articles in New York City have stirred public awareness regarding growing proven and alleged cases of elder abuse, mainly in institutions of elder care. It is important for health care providers to be aware of the dynamics of aging, in order to conduct thorough physical examinations and take careful histories to avoid overlooking elder abuse. Healthcare providers themselves need to be cognizant of their own attitudes towards the elderly or the aging process if they are to deliver unbiased care to the elderly.

CHAPTER TWO
LITERATURE REVIEW

This chapter will review literature pertaining to past research on the topics of elder abuse, neglect, and maltreatment. The literature was gathered from newspaper articles, textbooks, nursing and geriatric magazines, and other writings on the topic. Most of the literature is in the form of historical data. The literature cited will discuss the following:

- Who are the likely victims?
- Who are the abusers, along with penalties?
- Likely places where abuse takes place.
- Reporting elderly abuse, neglect, and maltreatment.
- Statistics proving increase of the problem.
- What can be done to prevent the problem?
- Assessing the elderly for signs of abuse neglect and maltreatment.
- Future predictions regarding aging and elderly abuse.
- Summary of chapter two.

WHO ARE THE LIKELY VICTIMS?

In the Journal of the American Medical Association (JAMA), April 1988, Dr. Greg Sachs, doing his residency at a geriatric care center, told of his experience in treating a grossly abused elderly patient. He told of an eighty-seven-year-old woman that was transferred from a hospital to the facility. She was admitted with multiple diagnoses:

- dementia
- pressure sores
- incontinence.
- diabetes
- anemia
- malnutrition
- multiple fractures

She was bed-bound. She responded only to painful stimuli. She had a foley bedside, continuous urinary drainage, and a gastrostomy tube for feeding. This woman's albumin level was abnormally low and her temperature was sub-normal. He mentioned that the patient was admitted to the hospital three months prior to her transfer to the geriatric unit. The reason for her admission to the hospital was hypoglycemic coma.

The doctor told of his introduction to the elderly lady. He placed a hand on her shoulder and reassuringly told her that he was going to examine her to see what he could do to help her. As he touched her, she screamed. As he proceeded to examine her, he came upon an open wound on her right hip, which was supposedly debrided by the doctors at the hospital. As he looked closer at the wound, he thought he saw some movement in it. He said he wondered if there were maggots inside. He looked closer but saw no maggots. The doctor soon realized that he was in fact seeing his own reflection in the shiny artificial prosthesis that was placed at the head of her femur during a previous surgery.

He remarked, "It seems to mirror the topsy-turvy medical care given to many patients." He told how her medical record showed "innumerable" lab tests and other procedures done; yet it was evident from her bedsores that she was not turned frequently, so that she developed the bedsores. In further comments on the elderly patient's case, the doctor said, "All of us are part of the human community, no matter how demented, contracted, or incontinent. Debilitated and dependent patients need us to reach out and care for them most, when we are starting to push them away. It is our distancing of ourselves from these people that is the true dehumanizing act...please, Lord, do not let me die with pressure sores." (Sachs, Greg A., *A Piece of My Mind: On Deeper Reflection. JAMA*, April 8, 1988).

Lawenstein, A., *Elder Abuse*, 1995, conducted a workshop on elder abuse in Isreal. He found that "persons at risk of abuse were either the lonely aged who are exposed to abuse by outside helpers or nursing cases who are bound to the home, many of whom suffer from some form of dementia." This finding could also be related to elder abuse in many other societies."

WHO ARE THE ABUSERS?
In their effort to expose perpetrators of elderly abuse, neglect, and maltreatment in nursing homes in New York State, Thomas Zambito and Joe Calderone, writers for the *New York Daily News*, wrote several articles. Some of the headlines are the following.
- "Medical Payments Help Foot Hefty Salaries, Records Show." (July 31, 2000)
- "Commish (Commissioner) Responds: 'We're on Nursing Home Case.'" (December 22, 2000)

- "New York Hit on Nursing Homes: State Inspectors Missed Violations" (Jan. 2000)
- "Feeling No Pain: Nursing Homes: State Inspectors Missed Violations" (Jan. 2000)
- "Milking The Helpless: Attorneys Siphoning Off Millions from the Elderly They Have Sworn to Protect." (May 20, 2000)
- 5 L.I. (Long Island) Nurses: Charges Cover-up of Patient Abuse." (November 7, 2000)
- "Cover-up Abuse-case Focus: Long Island Nursing Home at Center of Charges." (Feb. 15, 2001)

Thomas Zambito recently wrote the following article in the *New York Times*:

"Cover-up Abuse Case Focus" (January, 2000). This article told of two cover-up abuse cases in a nursing home in New York City.

One case was that of an eighty-six-year-old nursing home patient who fell one night and fractured her right hip and bruised her right shoulder. The nursing staff did nothing until next morning, when a new shift of nurses' aides came on duty. The patient's daughter stated that her mother's lips were bleeding because she bit them due to the pain she was feeling during the night. The patient was taken to the emergency room, where it was diagnosed that she had a compound fracture of her right hip. She died one month later. Five nurses were indicted for this case. The patient's daughter has filed a $20 million lawsuit. The charge against the nurses was falsification of medical records to cover up mistakes. The article went on to say that the same nurses were also charged in the death of another ninety-seven-year-old woman who authorities said was given her tube feeding by an enema bag instead of a feeding bag. This caused the patient to receive food that should run over ten hours in one hour.

The article pointed out that the former Director of Nursing and the Nursing Supervisor ordered a nurse to rewrite her nurse's notes to cover up the evidence of wrongdoing.

MEDICAID FAT CATS

Tom Zambito and Joe Calderone, *New York Daily News*. (July 31, 2000). The article pointed out that nursing home owners are using Medicaid payments to help foot their million dollar projects each year. Five nursing home owners in New York were said to make over one million in salaries. According to the writers, some owners put their relatives on their payrolls giving them six figure salaries in small nursing homes. The Sate Health Department issued a statement in which they said, "Nursing home owners even want more money to line their pockets." The article went on to say that federal officials cite nursing home staff shortages as the reason for increase in serious patient problems, including malnutrition and bedsores that lead to hospitalization.

DA SAYS NURSE WITHHELD PATIENTS' DRUGS, NEW YORK

Calderone, J and Zambito, T., *Daily News* (August 14, 2000), gave a report from the District Attorney's office. The article told of a temporary nurse on the night shift in a nursing home who failed to administer twenty-three medications to eleven of the forty-six frail elderly patients for whom she had to care. She falsified the patients' records to show that she gave the medications. Some of the patients involved had heart conditions and Parkinson's disease. Some needed tranquilzers, according to the article. The writers also stated that during an interview regarding the claim, one worker told the reporter that the nursing home was understaffed and needed equipment. The nurse was charged with twenty-three counts of willful violation of health laws and twenty-three counts of falsifying business records, as the article outlined.

T. Zambito, J Calderone and R. Buettner wrote an article in the *New York Daily News*, (May 20, 2001) which pointed out that certain lawyers and judges whom the court appoints as guardians for some senior citizens are taking millions of dollars in fees from the assets of some frail elderly citizens. The article told that since 1993, some attorneys and judges in New York have been paid at least sixty-three million dollars in fees from money of elderly people whose money they agreed to protect. The writers claim that nursing homes and hospitals sometimes seek guardians to be appointed so that those guardians can apply for Medicaid on behalf of the elderly. Before the elderly can be eligible for Medicaid their private money must be spent down. A previous article told of misappropriation of medical funds in some nursing homes. Another example of abusers, an article "Nursing Home Suit in Bogus Surgeries" was written by Bill Sanderson, *New York Post* (March 10, 2000). The article tells of a lawsuit against a nursing home for allowing doctors to perform unnecessary prostate surgery on twenty-four mentally disabled men. In writing about elderly abuse in Isreal, Owenstein A., *Elder Abuse; International and Cross-Cultural Perspective*, 1995, wrote the following: "The data reported to the chief welfare officers shows that a large number of perpetrators in the community are sons living with and caring for an elderly parent, usually a widowed mother who is at least seventy-five. Many of these sons suffer from various mental problems, retardation, or other chronic physical or mental conditions. Many are alcohol or drug users. Taking care of the older parent poses a burden the child cannot handle, which leads to incidents of abuse. The most common forms of abuse are financial and physical abuse." The author drew similarity from data by Quinn and Tonia (1986) and Kosberg (1988) that showed sons as the main perpetrators of abuse of the elderly in their own homes.

The Likely Places Where Elder Abuse Takes Place

Mike Amon and Tom Zambito writing in the *Daily News* (Thursday, February 15, 2001) "Nursing Home Deaths Soar" pointed out that the number of deaths in nursing homes in New York City are increasing.

They compared the number of deaths, 3,891 in 1990 to 6,475 in 1999, an increase of 66 percent as disclosed by the New York City Health Department. They mentioned several factors that could be responsible for the increase such as the following:

- Early discharges from hospitals due to rising hospital bills.
- Fewer people are taking care of dying relatives at home.
- Older people are going into nursing homes.

In 1985 the average age was eighty-five while in 2001 the average age is ninety.

In the article, Brant Fries, a professor at the University of Michigan's Institute of Gerontology, who is studying the characteristics of nursing home patients for the Federal Health and Human Services Department, pointed out that nursing homes are reimbursed at a higher rate for the sickest, closer to death, who require most care. These include those on ventilators and tube feedings, who require more care. Mr. Fries feels that nursing homes choose their category of patients who can bring more reimbursement. On the other hand, nursing home industry officials in disagreement with Mr. Fries say the increase is due to the increased demand for nursing home care. In the article, Amy Molino, a spokeswoman for the New York State Health Facilities Association, claims that the increase stems from the fact that nursing home census has increased, thereby increasing the number of nursing home deaths. The writers further compared the national nursing home deaths with those of the city of New York as the following: nationally, the number of deaths in 1990 was 347,559. In 1998 the total was 509,752. This showed an increase of 47 percent compared with New York City there has been an increase of 19 percent above the national average.

The article pointed out that experts claim that nursing homes are adapting themselves to unique case mix which results in a large number of poor including the elderly living on government programs like Medicaid and those with AIDS.

The article points out further that the number of nursing home beds in New York City has increased from fifty to sixty thousand over the past ten years but the writers feel that this alone is not responsible for the increase of deaths in New York Nursing Homes.

In an advertisement for Seeger Weiss, LLP in the *New York Daily News* (November 11, 2000), the following was written: "Nursing Home Alert. It is estimated that 35,000 Americans die each year due to neglect and abuse, bedsores, bruises, and sudden weight loss. If you suspect that your loved one has been the victim of neglect and abuse in a nursing home, ask questions and demand answers."

Normal aging differs from culture to culture. Normal aging differs from pathological aging by an absence of physical and mental diseases. Normal aging can be anomalous. For example: when an elderly person moves to a retirement home, this is neither pathological nor normal. Up to 1980, normal aging in the United States involved no disabilities with chronic or acute diseases. On the other hand, aging people who are disabled and poor and who cannot meet their needs are experiencing pathological aging.

New environments or changes can confront the elderly with a disturbance in their ability to use learned habits to deal with everyday living. This is the reason that middle-aged and older people are sometimes resistant to changing households or moving to different environments.

REPORTING ELDERLY ABUSE

George G. Pozgar in *Legal Aspects of Health Care Administration*, Seventh Edition, 1999 wrote on Elder Abuse. He pointed out that most states, including the District of Columbia, have enacted statutes regarding adult protective services laws that require mandatory reporting of elder abuse. He went on to say that a report by the Senate Subcommittee on elderly abuse told that elder abuse is less likely to be reported than child abuse. In comparing child abuse reporting with elder abuse reporting, he showed that one in three cases of child abuse are reported in contrast to one in eight cases of elder abuse that are reported.

Under this topic he mentioned the result of a major study on resident abuse in nursing homes that was conducted by the Office of Evaluations and Inspection, which is one of the three major offices within the office of the Inspector General. The result revealed that nearly all the participants who responded indicated that elder abuse is a problem in nursing homes.

The study showed that physical and emotional neglect and verbal and financial abuse were identified as the most prevalent forms of abuse. The abusers were identified as nursing home staff, medical personnel, other patients, families, or visitors. Nurse's aides and orderlies were shown to be the primary abusers in all types of abuse except for medical neglect. The author pointed out that it is proven that nursing home residents often do not report incidents of abuse due to fear of retaliation from abusers and difficulty in proving their claims.

The list of persons mentioned in health care who are required to report child abuse are also the same who can report elder abuse. Those mentioned on the list are:

- Physicians
- Administrators

- Interns
- Registered nurses
- Social Service Workers
- Chiropractors
- Dentists
- Psychologists
- Osteopaths
- Optometrists
- Mental Health Professionals
- Podiatrists
- Volunteers in nursing homes and other elderly residential facilities

In addition to this list, any concerned person may make the report. M. Robin Morris, RN, JD, wrote an article, "Elder Abuse; What the Law Requires." in August 1998 issue of *R.N. Magazine*. The article started off by pointing out that child abuse and the mistreatment of older people have prompted legislative (government) intervention into the problem. All states now have to protect older, vulnerable adults from abuse, neglect, and financial exploitation.

The article mentioned that for nurses to uphold their "legal and ethical obligations" to help stop elder abuse, they must know what constitutes abuse and what the reporting requirements are. The information was given under the following subheadings:
- The many forms of victimization
- Your duty to report
- Setting the process in motion

THE MANY FORMS OF VICTIMIZATION
Here the different forms of elder abuse and exploitation were defined and explained. These involved what constitutes physical abuse (including inappropriate use of drugs and other chemical or physical restraints) and psychological abuse.

YOUR DUTY TO REPORT
The author stated that the majority of the states require nurses and other health care professionals to report cases of suspected abuse, also that those states that did not mandate reporting of cases encourage it. "A reasonable belief that a person is abused or is likely to be abused is mentioned as the standard for reporting."

Grounds for suspecting abuse such as multiple bruises, evasiveness of caregivers, and other examples were outlined. The article mentioned that most sates give immunity from criminal and civil liability against reports as long as report of abuse was done in good faith. South Carolina was pointed out as a state that prohibits employers from taking action against employees that report abuse.

REFERENCE

1. Ramsay-Dlawsnik, H (1996) *Assessing Physical and Sexual Abuse in Health care settings.* In L.A. Baumhover and S.C. Beall (*Abuse Neglect of Older persons* pp 67-87) Baltimore Health Professionals Press.
2. Steigel, L.A. (1995) *Recommending Guidelines for State Courts Handling Cases Involving Elder Abuse.* Washington D.C. American Bar Association.

SETTING THE PROCESS

The article pointed out that each state has its own abuse reporting process. Most states require that the initial report should be made to a specific individual in the facility. This individual is responsible for forwarding the report to an agency or individual such as Adult Protective Service (APS), Long Term Care Ombudsman, or the police. Some policies require that the nurse or doctor should make the report. It also stated that if the suspected person is a health care provider, the report might also be reported to the licensing agency orally or in writing. This is done within twenty-four hours of the occurrence or the next business day. The agency to which the report was made is then expected to investigate the report in a timely manner. Careful documentation of details regarding the incident is very important. The article warns about drawing conclusions along with other guidelines for reporting. In the article the author also mentioned that some states would not share the result of investigation with the reporter.

The writer concluded by saying that elder abuse is an "ugly crime" which initially may be easy to dismiss from the observer's concern, but warns that from a legal and moral standpoint, looking the other way is not an option.

Suzanne Wolfe, editor for *RN Magazine* (1998), wrote an article "Looking for Signs of Abuse" in the August 1998 issue of *RN Magazine*. In bold print she emphasized "As America Ages" and "Growing old shouldn't mean becoming a victim but for too many of this country's senior citizens it does." The article carried the picture of an elderly gray-haired lady with a look of depression on her face. She then proceeded to give advice on how nurses can help prevent abuse to elders. She first pointed out that it is believed that over one million Americans age sixty or older are victims of abuse in domestic settings each year. She also confirmed that the full number is not known due to underreporting, but that some experts believe that only one case in fourteen is ever reported.

The reasons she cited were:
1. Many victims do not want to report the abuse due to
   Shame
   Fear
2. A sense of loyalty to their abusers
Clinicians sometimes do not think of the possibility of abuse and overlook the presenting signs.

The article continued that all too often the signs of abuse are passed off as related to the normal aging process. An example given was recurrent fractures that are frequently attributed to osteoporosis that occurs in the elderly, especially women. The author outlined the risk factors and advised on how to investigate for abuse, also on what can be done to stop abuse.

The following sub headings were used:
1. Profiling victims and abusers.
2. When to suspect mistreatment.
3. Asking questions to uncover some answers.
4. How to intervene to protect the patient.

Jogerst, Gerald J. at al. "Community Characteristics Associated with Elder Abuse." *Journal of the American Geriatric Society* (2000) conducted a study in which they gave important statistics regarding elder abuse and community characteristics.

The article stated, "Studies of the U.S. Population has estimated the annual prevalence of elder abuse to range from 700,000 to 2.5 million. Reported cases of elder abuse in 1991 were up to 94 percent from 1986. Of the report investigators substantiated 54 percent. A total of 551,011 older persons experienced abuse, neglect, and/or self neglect in the home setting in 1996. Of this total, Adult Protective Services Substantiated 21 percent.

Reports from sentinels regarding trained individuals in a variety of community agencies, who have frequent contact with the elderly documented, the remaining 435,901 (79 percent) not reported to Adult Protective Services."

The article went on to say that from these National Elder Abuse Incidence Study figures, it can be estimated that almost four times more new cases of elder abuse and mistreatment were unreported than the number that was substantiated by Adult Protective Services.

The following disclosures were also given.
1. Family members reported 20 percent of the substantiated reports of domestic elder abuse, neglect, and mistreatment.
2. Hospitals made 17.3 percent of reports.
3. Home care providers made 9.6 percent of reports.
4. Physicians, nurses, and clinics made 8.4 percent of reports. A study in Michigan showed that between 1989 and 1993 physician reporting

rates were highest in counties with low physician to population ratios. This shows that rural primary care physicians are better at detecting and reporting elder abuse, neglect, and mistreatment.

WHAT CAN BE DONE TO PREVENT ELDERLY ABUSE, NEGLECT, AND MALTREATMENT

Joan E. Bowers, RN, in the article "Caring for the Elderly," in *RN Magazine* of January 1978, gave very positive guidelines for caring for the elderly, in order to avoid detecting abuse, neglect, and maltreatment. The advice is useful both for caregivers in domestic settings as well as in institutions that provide care for the elderly.

She started off by pointing out hostility, incontinence, and insomnia as three of the main problems that are common among elderly people. Reference was made to a case where a nurse was passing through a crowded patient waiting room. She recognized an elderly patient, Mr. Green, to whom she said hello. She did not wait for his response. Mr. Green would only raise his hand. He evidently had a speech impairment and was unable to respond spontaneously. The response only came audible after the nurse was gone. The author feels that nurses are sometimes too busy to give patients a chance to respond or explain. Whenever this happens, speech impairment or aphasia is sometimes mistaken for confusion and could lead to neglect. The author feels that such patients need to be given time to try to communicate even with hand gestures. If this does not happen, it could cause frustration or confusional psychosis in the elderly person.

The author warned against stereotyping the elderly as a homogenous group. Instead the article points out that many are "clear-minded and able to take care of their own needs, as well as those who are frequently confused or physically disabled." In other words each elderly must be treated individually according to his or her own needs.

Certain guidelines are given for dealing with some of the common conditions affecting the elderly such as:

- Combating incontinence.
- Wrestling with insomnia.
- Handling hostility.
- Empathizing with emotions.

COMBATING INCONTINENCE

Instead of applying diapers or indwelling catheters, which can sometimes do more harm than good, several practical steps or measures can be taken to maintain dignity and prevent urinary tract infection in the elderly person. If an indwelling catheter must be inserted, it must be removed after two to

three days. Otherwise, this could lead to urinary tract infection or iatrogenic infection:
1. Provide access to bathroom if patient is able.
2. Remove bedside rails if the elderly person does not need them.
3. Place urinal within reach.
4. Place call bell within reach.
5. Place a special mark or color on the bathroom door for easy recognition.
6. Try to assess the degree of confusion, if any.
7. Practice route to the bathroom with the elderly person.
8. Provide a night-light for the bathroom.
9 .Provide wall-safety rails.
10. Try to find out when the elderly person is most likely to void, and try to chart a pattern. Try to get help for the elderly person at such times. In other words place the person on a toileting program.

WRESTLING WITH INSOMNIA

One of the main causes of insomnia is lack of exercise. The author feels that daytime napping could be a common reason for insomnia.

The advice given for this:
- Take walks outdoors.
- Even sit up in bed.
- Back rubs.
- Warm milk, a snack, or a glass of wine before bedtime.
- A bath before bedtime.
- Avoid going to sleep too early.
- Activity during the day.
- Mild sedation e.g.: Sparine or Chloral hydrate on doctor's advice.
- Barbiturates should be avoided.

The author gives reminder that the elderly person can become confused or hostile if he or she awakes before the effect of the sedative drugs wear off.

HANDLING HOSTILITY

Elderly people who are hostile, aggressive, or obstinate may be suffering from organic brain syndrome, depression, or anxiety and may be under doctor's treatment for these conditions. Sometimes certain tranquilizers tend to make the condition worse. If this is suspected, the doctor should be notified.

The author (Joan Bowers) feels that many times human contact and understanding is helpful. For example allowing independence or making the environment uncomplicated. A quiet place in the home can eliminate the use of tranquilizers.

EMPATHIZING WITH EMOTIONS

The author feels that the first thing to do when an elderly person goes to live with a family member or to a nursing home is to try to obtain information on their previous lifestyle and idiosyncrasies. For example, an elderly person in the nursing home may have a hearing impairment and have no hearing aid. The suggestion is to put the earpieces of the caregiver's stethoscope in the ears while the caregiver speaks slightly louder in the chest piece. Refer to audiologist.

Other Advice:

Help them to feel at home.

In a nursing home, husband and wife should share the same room. If only one is a patient, the other should be allowed to visit. They should be allowed privacy. The author feels that all elderly people should be treated as adults, regardless of their state or condition, whether in a relative's home or in a nursing home. The elderly person should be given the assurance that he or she is not abandoned and that there is always some caring person available for them. Above all, the elderly should be treated with honesty, truth, fairness, and respect.

WHAT CAN BE DONE TO PREVENT ELDER ABUSE

Walt Duka, in his article "OAA (Older American ACT) A Major Exception; Hill Deadlock Stalls Key Bills" *AARP Bulletin* (December 2000), wrote on the approval of the new Older Americans Act Bill.

The article stated that after five years of hard work by the AARP volunteers, members, staff, and others concerned with aging, the senate approved the authorization of the Older Americans' Act by a bi-partisan vote of 94-0.

The act is said to be very important to American families. It is a federally funded program. The following are the senior citizens program that fall under the OAA.

- Senior Citizens centers
- Meals on Wheels
- Legal Assistance Service
- Ombudsman Affirmation
- Employment Services
- National Family Caregiver Support Program

The Programs help to promote:

- Nutrition
- Employment training
- Community Service Opportunities
- Protection against abuse
- Support for families providing care to their elderly

The article further disclosed that the legislation (HR782), which President Clinton signed on November 13, 2000, creates a new National

Family Caregiver program and authorizes $125 million for funding. The money will be distributed to provide caregiving training, counseling, respite care, peer support, and other assistance that will benefit the elderly. Under the column "News View" of *Geriatric Nursing*, March/April 1997, an unnamed columnist wrote a short article titled "Government of Singapore Requires Citizens to Support Aging Parents." It stated that there is a new legislation in effect in Singapore known as "Maintenance of Parents." The legislation requires citizens of Singapore to financially support their elderly parents who are in need. It further discussed that the law went into effect in June 1996 and that by September of that year, a matter of three months, there were already more than one hundred parents who filed suits against their children. The law gives parents over sixty years of age the right to sue their children for assistance. According to demographic projections, the number of Singaporeans over age sixty will quadruple by the year 2020.

With this fast rate of aging of citizens in Singapore, the total elderly will be 26 percent of the population by the year 2020, as mentioned in the article.

The importance of a good parent/child relationship will be further discussed later in this book. A good parent/child relationship developed early between patents and their children could prevent the need for legislation of such laws in many countries. Here in the United States the government gives a certain amount of assistance to needy adult children who care for their elderly parents, through the Department of Social Services under the Older Americans Act Programs.

Smith, Margaret K. and Sullivan, Jean M, "Nurses Perception on Most Important Caring Behaviors in a Long Term Care Setting" *Geriatric Nursing*, March to April 1997.

The article gave the following tips to nursing staff who works with the elderly:

- Check on patients frequently.
- Give quick response to patient's calls.
- Encourage patients to call for help if they have problems.
- Teach patients to care for themselves if they are able.
- Be cheerful.
- Listen to patients.
- Involve patients and significant others in their plan of care.
- Realize that nights are the most difficult time for elderly patients.
- Speak to patients in understandable language.
- Encourage patients to ask questions they might have.
- Have a consistent approach with patients.
- Get to know patients as individuals.
- Be calm with patients.
- Know when to call the doctor.

- Give good physical care.
- Help patients establish realistic goals.
- Offer reasonable alternatives to patients: Example, when to bathe or shower them etc.
- Touch patients when they need comforting.
- Talk to patients.
- Get to know patients' relatives.

WHAT CAN BE DONE TO PREVENT ELDERLY ABUSE?

The following articles address the above topic:
1. Cosner, Edward, et. al. "Senior Care Or Nightmare?" *New York Daily News*, Editorial, November 14, 2000.
2. Vallone, Peter F. "A View From the City." *Caribbean Life, Brooklyn and Staten Island Edition*. The future for Seniors in New York City, January 9, 2001.
3. Novello, Antonio C. "Commish (Commissioner) Responds: We're on Nursing Home Case."

SENIOR CARE OR NIGHTMARE

In this article, Edward Kosner, et. al., commented that nursing home care would increase as the population ages. At the present rate of aging, abuse of the elderly will increase also. They also commented on the case of the ninety-seven-year-old woman who in one hour was fed a volume of feed that should have been delivered in ten hours by the substitution of an enema bag for the standard feeding bag. The patient died after uncontrolled vomiting. They referred to the act as "sickening contempt and appalling betrayal of patient trust." The article mentioned that Jose Midland, Director of the State Attorney General's Medicaid Fraud Control Unit, said, "Not since the dark days of New York nursing home scandal of the mid 1970s has my office seen such a betrayal of patient trust...."

They felt that patient trust is betrayed in some nursing homes, but the problem is to find out which nursing homes are doing something about it. The article further disclosed that Maldonado's Office reported that complaint of abuse in nursing homes had increased by 45 percent in the first six months of the year 2000. He termed this "alarming and disturbing." In examining this finding, Mr. Maldonado said that this might not only be an increase in elderly abuse but an increase in reporting. He felt that better reporting could be more beneficial. He further stated, "If complaints are not filed, sadistic staffers who let patients suffer can continue to operate unchecked." He concluded by saying, "A society is judged by the way it cares for its old. So far this society is failing miserably."

Valone, Peter F., "A View From the City; The Future for Seniors in New York City." *Caribbean Life*, (Brooklyn and Staten Island edition) January 9, 2001, Council Speaker Peter Valone made reference to New York City as the "Ultimate Retirement City." The report said the city council respects the fact that senior citizens are the fastest growing group of the population.

Plans for seniors include:
- Establishment of fourteen retirement communities.
- Weekend Food Program ($6 million funding).
- Social Workers in Senior Center ($2.5 million).
- Transportations Program ($.5 million).
- Handyman Program ($.5 million).
- Nursing Homes:

Mr. Vallone stated that despite the above programs, 5 percent of seniors will live in nursing homes. The problem of untrained, underpaid, inadequate governmental supervision and regulation will be addressed. He concluded by saying, "We owe our elders everything including the best quality of life…to improve the lives of nursing home residents."

- Commish (Commissioner) responds: "We're on Nursing Home Case." Dr. Antonia Novello, State Health Commissioner in the above article in the *Daily News* of December 22, 2000, mentioned his concerns of previous articles decrying elderly abuse in nursing homes.

He gave public reassurance that the respect, dignity, and quality of life for New York's elderly are top priority in his department. The following are some actions to be taken by his department:
- Sanctions and fines for offenders.
- Greater staffing.
- Better training.
- Reports of survey findings to the public through web sites, etc.
- $89 million, to train and attract health care workers.
- Improve surveillance staff for the Health Department.

ATCHLEY, ROBER C. A CONTINUING THEORY OF NORMAL AGING

The author began by saying that continuity is an "illusive concept." He explained that on one hand it can mean to remain unchanged, uniform, homogeneous, or humdrum; on the other hand, it could mean a basic structure which is persistent but allows for changes within the basic structure. The basic structure is coherent. The parts of this structure allow one to differentiate it from others. Middle aged and older adults attempt to preserve and maintain their lifestyles by applying familiar strategies to familiar arenas of their lives. Overall the community theory holds that in making adaptive choices, middle aged and older adults attempt to preserve and maintain existing internal and external structures by using strategies tied to their past experiences of themselves and their social world. Change is linked to the person's perceived past. It continued that continuity is therefore an adaptive strategy that is promoted by individual preferences and social approval.

For caregivers to understand the effect of change in the life of an elderly person, who leaves his familiar surrounding and adapt to institutional life, Robert C. Atchly explains. "It is important for care givers to understand the continuity theory of normal aging in order to effectively help older people adjust to changes. Lack of understating of the aging process could sometimes result in abuse, neglect, and maltreatment of elderly persons."

ASSESSING FOR SIGNS OF ABUSE, NEGLECT, AND MALTREATMENT

Staton-Novac, Debra A. "Seven Keys to Assessing The Elderly." *Nursing 88*, August 1988, gave practitioners the following systematic keys to consider and follow, when assessing the elderly, in order to rule out abuse, neglect, and maltreatment.

1. Chief concerns of elderly person
2. Health History
3. Medication History
4. Recent Life Changes
5. Daily Activities
6. Cognitive Patterns
7. Support Systems

In some of the keys the author gave scenarios or short case histories as illustrations.

In introducing the article the author gave the following case history. A seventy-five-year-old patient was hospitalized with history of abdominal distension and pain. Three days after admission, his temperature became subnormal and he became confused. An exploratory laparotomy revealed a ruptured appendix which led to peritonitis. This patient's confusion stemmed from the infection of his peritoneal cavity. Other reasons for confusion could be malnutrition, senility, anemia, endocrine disorders (e.g. diabetes, cardiovascular disorders, adverse drug reaction, or some neurological disorders). The author mentions that there may be as many as one hundred documented causes of confusion in the elderly.

The following seven steps were given for structuring assessment in order to arrive at meaningful results or findings.

1) Chief concerns:

The first step is to ascertain the reason for seeking health care because the elderly don't always show typical signs and symptoms of disease.

The primary question to find out from the elderly patient or any family member or anyone accompanying him or her is why the patient is seeking health care.

Other questions to explore are:
- What new health changes have been observed?
- How have the changes affected the elderly?
- When did the changes begin?

2) Health History

It was pointed out that there is an increase in hospitalization of elderly people. A careful history is important, especially in cases of recurrent injury or illness that require further investigation. The author pointed out that these cases often reveal situations of physical or psychological abuse, financial hardship, or intolerance of certain treatments. Another possible problem could be misunderstanding of certain medication or treatments as in the case of the elderly patient who was placed on a new antihypertensive medication that caused her to fall and fracture her hip. It was pointed out that there is an increase in hospitalization of elderly people. A careful history is important especially in case of recurrent injury or illness that require further investigation.

3) Medication History

The author (Debrah A. Staton-Novac) pointed out that it is a known fact that elderly people take a lot of both prescription and over-the-counter drugs. Therefore they are liable to have adverse medication reactions. An example was given of a patient who went to the Emergency Room because of difficulty in urinating. It was later discovered that he was taking the drug Norpace or Dispyramide which can cause bladder tone impairment. Another patient who was taken to Emergency Department in a hypoglycemic coma was discovered to have taken the drug Inderal for hypertension, along with Diabinese or Chlorpropamide for diabetes. The Inderal had masked the signs and symptoms of hypoglycemia. Elderly people frequently take antacids for indigestion, painkillers for arthritis, and cough medication. Some of these can have adverse reactions to prescription medications. Included was a medication questionnaire for elderly patients that were recommended for use when doing medication history assessment. A fairly recent discovery is that the intake of grapefruit juice can cause adverse reaction with certain systemic drugs. Elderly patients should be discouraged from taking grapefruit juice, so as to avoid adverse reaction with medication.

4) Recent Life Changes

One theory pointed out that any kind of significant life changes, whether good or bad, can cause stress. This is very important with elderly people who frequently experience death of a spouse or other loved ones or separation from family. An example is going to live in an elder care facility. The case given was an elderly patient who recently lost her spouse before she was hospitalized twice due to malnutrition. It was later learnt that she had lost interest in preparing her meals. Through a social worker, she was encouraged to join a senior citizens club and to resume her interest in music.

5) Daily Activities

Some factors to consider in this area are physical activities, eating habits, toileting, and sleeping. By looking for patterns in daily activities, problems could be identified. Ambulation should also be considered.

To illustrate the importance of probing daily activities the author uses the following case: The family of an elderly male reported that he had lost interest in gardening, and he was tired easily. He was diagnosed with hypothyroidism.

6) Cognitive Patterns

Confusion and depression are very common in the elderly. These may result from different conditions, such as certain drug toxicity. Digoxin and theophyillin are among these drugs, as experienced by a ninety-year-old patient who developed digoxin toxicity which cased confusion. Drug toxicity is said to be the cause of up to 50 percent of confusion and depression in the elderly as outlined by the author.

In assessing cognitive patterns, the author suggested the following:
- Review recent stressful life changes and current medication regimen.
- Focus on the patient's reasoning ability, memory, and orientation. "Reasoning ability is the best indication of intellectual function." The author gave examples of questions that may be asked to assess the above.
- Investigate any recent changes in behavior, mood, and activities.

7) Support System

Evaluation of the elderly person's support system is very important. For example: someone to assist with activities of daily living, someone to visit, safe housing arrangement, or social involvement such as church or senior citizens group. An example of the importance of investigating support system was the case of a ninety-one-year-old lady who lived alone and was taking a diuretic. She did not drink enough liquids. This led to dehydration which caused two hospitalizations in the same summer. Members of her church started to visit and assist, along with the visiting nurse.

FUTURE PREDICTIONS REGARDING AGING AND ELDER ABUSE

Anthony R. Kovner and Steven Jones, authors of *Health Care Delivery in the United States, Sixth Edition* 1999, wrote on the future of aging and ethnic changes in the population. They predicted that the continuing aging American population will command much attention among policy makers and health care providers over the next thirty years. At present 47 percent of hospital admissions in the United States are over age sixty-five. This accounts for 13 percent of the population.

The study predicted that the number of elderly persons age sixty-five and over in the society will double in the next twenty-five years. The fast aging rate will exert more demands for various types of health care, especially care that relates to chronic illnesses and support services for the frail elderly. The aging growth rates are highest among the eldest of the old. No percentage was given for the group.

The authors pointed out that while there is an increase in the aging group, there is a continuous shrinkage of the informal support system. The number of adults age twenty-one to sixty-five (the main workforce age group of the informal care giver) is expected to decrease from 12.5 per elderly person over 75 in 1980 to 6.5 per elderly person in 2025 (according to a report by the US Census Bureau, 1992). Another important population shift identified is the rapid increase of ethnic diversity. For example those of Asian and Pacific Islands origin will increase from nine million in 1992 to forty-one million in 2050, according to Brownson and Kreauter, 1997 and US Census Bureau 1992. With these statistics it is of utmost importance that abuse of elders be controlled as soon as possible.

CONCLUSION OF CHAPTER 2

The literature review involved addressed all aspects of the study.
For example:

- Who are the victims?
- Who are the abusers?
- Likely places where abuse takes place.
- Reporting elderly abuse neglect and maltreatment.
- Statistics: The statistics that were involved support the hypothesis that elder abuse is increasing.
- What can be done to prevent the problem: Joan Bowers did not only give advice on how to prevent abuse of the elderly but also gave pointers as to what can lead to vulnerability of elders who are abused.
- Assessing the elderly for signs of abuse, neglect, and maltreatment.
- The future of aging was outlined by Anthony R. Kovner and Steven Jonas. These predictions could point to serious problems for the elderly in the society if the present trend of abuse is not urgently curtailed.

Although a large proportion of elderly abusers are family members, it must still be stressed that many family members are very loving and caring to their elderly. This largely depends on cultural views on relationship to the elderly, an observation made by the researcher. Some families are attentive, loving, and kind to their elderly to the very end of life, while some will have their family members institutionalized and they are never seen or heard from again by their elders.

CHAPTER THREE
METHODOLOGY

This chapter will discuss the following:
   3.1 The Approach
   3.2 Survey Methods: What is a Questionnaire?
   3.3 Data Gathering Methods
   3.4 Data Base of Study
   3.5 The Questionnaire
       a.   Response Rate
       b.   Interpreting the Response to the Questionnaire
   3.6 Validity of Data
   3.7 Limitations of Study
   3.8 Sample Size
   3.9 Summary

METHODOLOGY

The data involved in the study came from both writings and observations. The kinds of data were both descriptive (questionnaire) and historical (the accounts given by different writers in the literature review).

The questionnaire was designed to mainly assess the effects of caregivers' attitudes on the care given to the elderly, the rate of reporting of abuse or suspected abuse, and whether or not there is an increase in elderly abuse.

The literature that was gathered was mainly to find answers to the questions of concern regarding elderly abuse that were mentioned in Chapter One.

THE APPROACH

Two approaches were involved: a descriptive survey approach and the use of historical data. In approaching the problem, the following steps were taken:
   •   Review of newspaper articles.
   •   Review of textbook accounts.

- Review of nursing magazines; long-term care magazines, geriatric magazines.
- Utilization of the medical library at University Hospital, Brooklyn, New York.
- Utilization of the main Brooklyn Public Library, New York.
- Use of a Long Term Care Facility.

SURVEY METHODS:

The survey methods are a) descriptive and b) historical. The descriptive method arises from participant observation. The participant observer is involved in daily operations of a Long Term Care Facility that includes care of the elderly. One of the functions of the participant observer is direct involvement in investigations of reported or suspected abuse of elderly by care givers. The main instrument employed was a questionnaire. All of the participants in the questionnaire work at the Long Term Care Facility where the questionnaire was generated and distributed. The historical data involved literature review of newspaper articles and other writings on elderly abuse, neglect, and maltreatment.

WHAT IS A QUESTIONNAIRE

A questionnaire is described as a commonplace instrument for observing data beyond the physical reach of the observer as explained by Leedy, Paul D., *Practical Research Planning and Design*, Second Edition, McMillian Press, 1980, page 99. An analogy used by the writer to describe a questionnaire is that "Data sometimes lie buried...or within the attitudes, feelings, or reactions of men and women...therefore the problem is to devise a tool to probe below the surface." The questionnaire is a personal means of gathering data.

DATA GATHERING METHOD

The data was gathered from libraries, textbooks, and concepts as well as observations gathered from the Long Term Care Facility in which the researcher works. The data involved in the study includes a questionnaire that was randomly distributed to a cross-section of the multidisciplinary staff of the facility.

DATA BASE OF STUDY

The database involved accounts by the writers for the *New York Daily* newspaper, especially the writings by Joe Caldrone and Thomas Zambeto. The writings were mostly critical and analytical in nature. They gave inside accounts of elder abuse, neglect, and maltreatment in some elder care facilities in New York State. The articles were gathered over a period of nine months. The textbooks involved were:

Pozner, George C., *Legal Aspects of Health Care Administration*, Seventh Edition, Aspen Publication, 1999.

Kover, Anthony A. and Steven Jonas, *Health Care Delivery in the United States*, Sixth Edition, Springer Publishing Co., 1998. The rest of the data was collected from nursing, geriatric long-term care, and medical magazines. Reports from the National Center on Elder Abuse, Washington D.C., *AARP Bulletin*, and *The Journal of the American Medical Association*. The self-composed questionnaire by the researcher is also a part of the database.

Many researchers have approached the problem from the victims' perspectives. This research is aimed mainly at examining the practitioner's views by asking questions that could give background information as to:

1. the reason for negative treatment of the elderly by some practitioners,
2. to assess the rate at which health care practitioners report elderly abuse, and
3. to assess if there is widespread increase in elderly abuse.

THE QUESTIONNAIRE

Through participant observation a questionnaire was developed. The questionnaire was distributed to a cross-section of employees who work at a Long Term Care Facility. The following were the purposes of the study:

1. To find an explanation of how employees perceive elderly patients/residents.
2. To possible explain the hypothesis that there is an increase in elderly abuse, neglect, and maltreatment.
3. To get an idea of the percentage of reporting of elderly abuse, neglect, and maltreatment.

THE QUESTIONS AND RESPONSES

The questionnaire was distributed to thirty racial-ethnically diverse employees comprised of doctors, nurses, nurses-aides, and orderlies. All individuals work in a Long Term Care Facility. At the end of one week, twenty-three questionnaires were collected. The following represents the questions and the responses.

Questions	Yes	No	Undecided
1. Have you ever thought of becoming old?	11=48%	9=39%	3=13%
2. Is your mother alive?	15=66%	8=33%	0

3. Is your father alive?   14=61%   9=39%   0

4. Did you grow up with your parents?   19=83%   4=16%   0

5. Are any of your parents or grand parents over age 65?   14=60%   9=39%   0

6. Is there an elderly person living in your home?   8=33%   15=66%   0

7. Do you like working with elderly patients?   9=39%   14=60%   0

8. Have you had training regarding elderly abuse, neglect, and maltreatment?   17=74%   6=26%   0

9. Do you feel that abuse of the elderly in Nursing Homes is increasing?   15=66%   4=16%   4=16%

10. If you witness or suspect abuse of an elderly person, would you report it?   9=39%   3=13%   11=48%

INTERPRETING THE RESPONSES TO THE QUESTIONNAIRE

Question 1
Have you ever thought of becoming old?
11 of the 23 who responded said yes, 9 responded no, and 3 were undecided. This was interpreted that a greater percentage of participants have concerns about becoming old.

Question 2
Is your mother alive?
15 of the 23 participants responded yes, 8 responded no. This was interpreted that 66 percent of the participants' mothers were alive. Another variable that could mean that 66 percent of the participants have a relationship with an older person than themselves.

Question 3
Is your father alive?
This was also interpreted that a larger percentage (61 percent) of the participants has a relationship with an older person than themselves.

Question 4
Did you grow up with your parents?
This was interpreted that a greater percentage (83 percent) of the participants have experienced parent/child bonding which also could be a variable in the attitudes towards older people.

Question 5
Are any of your parents or grandparents over age 65?
The response was interpreted that a greater percentage (61 percent) of the participants have a relationship with an elderly person of their own family. This is a variable that could influence their attitude towards the elderly with whom they work.

Question 7
Do you like working with elderly patients?
This was interpreted that a greater percentage (61 percent) of caregivers in this facility do not have a special liking for working with the elderly. The reason could be that they work with the elderly just to have a job. This is a variable that could also result in negative attitudes in the treatment of the elderly residents with whom they work.

Question 8
Have you had training regarding elder abuse, neglect, and maltreatment?
This response is interpreted that approximately 75 percent of the participants had training in elderly abuse, neglect, and maltreatment. This training is supposed to be mandatory for all practitioners in Long Term Care Facilities in New York and other states. This could be another variable that may be responsible for negative treatment and incidents of elderly abuse in that facility.

Question 9
Do you feel that abuse of the elderly is increasing?
This was interpreted that a greater percentage (65 percent) feel that abuse of the elderly is increasing. This question could have been confined to that facility because it is believed that elderly abuse in domestic settings is also on the increase.

Question 10
If you witness or suspect abuse of an elderly person, would you report it?
The highest percentage (48 percent) was undecided as to whether or not they would report abuse of the elderly. This result could relate to the high rate of underreporting of elder abuse.

VALIDITY OF DATA
The validity of the data in this study can be addressed from questions 8, 9, and 10 which deal with training that workers received, their perceptions of the increase of elderly abuse, and their professional responses if abuse is observed. The data in this study is supported by the findings of Calderone, Joe, "Nursing Home Allegations on the Rise," *New York Daily News*, August

1, 2000, since two-thirds of the participants in this study also agreed that abuse of the elderly is increasing. In addition, a report by an Ombudsman Program in Illinois (1999) revealed that in 1998 and 1999 there was actual harm to elderly in 31 percent of federally certified facilities compared to only 6 percent of facilities in 1995.

The 39 percent of positive responses to question #10 is also validated by the following:

A.) Dr. Charles E. Marshall, *Geriatrics Magazine*, 2000, states that only one in five or 20 percent of elderly abuse cases will be reported. He also pointed out that physicians report only 25 percent of all cases of elderly abuse.

B.) Dr. Fredrick Sherman in a round table discussion in *Geriatrics Magazine* (July 1992), when asked what he does about elder abuse when he thinks it exits, responded that, "...the only other option in dealing with these cases is to report the family to a government agency on a voluntary basis, which is the way it is done in New York State. However, I have not done this, because then I lose my relationship with the family."

C.) U.S. Congress, House Select Committee, 1980, reported that only one in six cases of abuse in the U.S.A. is reported.

D.) CNN Television, Channel 99, in commenting on an elderly abuse case on June 14, 2001 reported that the National Center on Elder Abuse reported that "the 800,000 cases recently reported is only a fraction of the whole."

SAMPLE SIZE

The ability to generalize from the findings is questionable due to the small size of the sample, but it could be used as an awareness tool in the facility where the study was conducted. This factor has been identified as the most common criticism in other researchers. For example, Shua-Haim and Gross (1996) did research to assess safety in driving on four Alzheimer's patients with their caretakers. They concluded that such old people are able to drive automobiles when accompanied. From that study, the researcher made recommendations to the Department of Motor Vehicles regarding devising driving guidelines and tests for older Alzheimer's motorists. The sample was too small for serious consideration of the recommendation.

LIMITATIONS OF STUDY

As one limitation, there are several writings on the topic of elder abuse which could easily cause the researcher to stray from the points being researched. In order to stay focused, the researcher had to bear the specific research problems in mind. Another limitation is the number of participants involved in the questionnaire. It is questionable whether the information gathered is enough to make an overall determination involving all the employees who work in the Long Term Care Facility where the study was conducted.

Summary of Chapter

The data involved in the research shows that elder abuse, neglect, and maltreatment in elder care facilities and in communities hinges on attitudes of caregivers. Another problem cited was probably ignorance regarding the dynamics of aging process.

From the result of the questionnaire and some of the literature reviewed, ex. Eckley, S.C.A. and Vilakazi, P.A.C., *Elder Abuse International and Cross-Cultural Perspectives: Elder Abuse in South Africa*, The Hawthorn Press, 1995, pp 171, it could be concluded that there is a multinational, multicultural, and multidisciplinary problem among some caregivers regarding their attitudes towards the elderly.

The result of the questionnaire seems to agree with some writers on the topic where attitude is concerned. With these facts in mind, it requires greater awareness and reshaping of the attitudes of caregivers towards the elderly, in order to prevent abuse, neglect, and maltreatment.

A follow-up of some of the elder abuse cases cited in the newspaper accounts show that some offenders have been brought to justice. The results of the findings from question 9 of the questionnaire support the hypothesis that elder abuse, neglect, and maltreatment is increasing.

Chapter Four

Data Analysis

The data analysis section of the study focused on the following:
a.   Limitations of the findings of the study.
b.   Limitations of the data.
c.   Areas of possible omissions.
d.   Reliability of data.
The data involved are used as evidence to support the hypotheses that:
1.   Elderly abuse, neglect, and maltreatment is increasing.
2.   Negative attitudes of elderly care practitioners contribute to the problems of elderly abuse, neglect, and maltreatment.
3.   There is a low rate of reporting of elderly abuse among practitioners.
4.   The findings of the questionnaire in data analysis of Chapter 3:
Of the 30 questionnaires that were distributed, 23=77 percent were collected. Results of the questionnaire were compiled on the data from the responses of the 23 that were collected.

Two problems were involved:
1.   A total of 18 participants=60 percent of the sample were undecided about their responses to 3 of the questions.
2.   7 of the participants (23 percent) of the sample refused to return the completed questionnaires.

The following are the questions on which participants were undecided:
1.   **Question 2**: Is your mother alive? A possible explanation could be that these employees could have been adopted or grew up in foster care, etc.
2.   **Question 9**: Do you feel that abuse of the elderly is increasing? The four participants or 16 percent who were undecided could have been among the caregivers who did not comply with the mandatory in-service training on elderly abuse, neglect, and mistreatment, since several areas of the study revealed that the problem is increasing.

3. **Question 10**: If you witness or suspect abuse of an elderly person would you report it? The 11 participants or 48 percent who were undecided could support the hypothesis that reporting is low among elderly care practitioners.

In summarizing the responses to the questionnaire, if the sample truly represented an overall response for all the workers in the Long Term Care Facility, the following facts would be evident:

- A greater percentage of workers have concerns regarding becoming old.
- Most workers have relationships with persons older than themselves.
- A greater percentage have experienced a parent/child relationship. This could help in maintaining a good relationship with elderly parents or patients.
- A greater percentage of workers in the facility do not necessarily like to work with the elderly. This could have negative impact on the quality of care and relationship with the elderly. This could also be grounds for elderly abuse, neglect, and maltreatment.

Other factors that could have influenced the result of the study include the sample size of 30 and the time allotted for completion. Even though simple and familiar terms were used in the constructions of the individual questions, there was no guarantee that the participants interpreted the questions as the researcher intended. Since the response rate was above 75 percent the researcher did not determine any more information that would explain the characteristics of the non-respondents or obtain their responses. With this in mind, the researcher did not consider the response rate to be seriously biased. Since the response rate of the participants was above 75 percent the researcher did not determine any bias in the representative sample.

VALIDITY

The researcher used the following questions to determine the validity of the questionnaire.

a. How important is the topic to the participants?

It was assumed that since the participants were active practitioners in the health care facility that their responses would be valid. It was also assumed that these individuals would be interested in the topic and that they were also informed about the conditions that were being studied.

b. Did the questionnaire protect the participants' anonymity?

The participants were not required to identify themselves; instead the researcher assigned a number to each participant. This again ensured the validity of the questionnaire.

RELIABILITY OF THE DATA

Several conditions would have to be used in order to ensure the reliability of this study. These would include building some redundancy into the questionnaire where some items could be re-phrased or repeated. However, this method is both expensive and time-consuming. If the study could be redesigned and the time constraints eliminated, it would be possible to employ these methods that would help to ascertain the reliability of the present study.

CHAPTER FIVE
SUMMARY, DISCUSSION,
RECOMMENDATIONS

This chapter will discuss the summary of the study, discussion of the findings, and recommendations for dealing with the problem of elderly abuse, neglect, and maltreatment. The study was designed to examine the problem of elderly abuse, neglect, and maltreatment.

1. Summary
    a) Specific findings.
    b) Implications of findings for the U.S. Health Care Delivery System.
        *   Health Care Cost.
        *   Culture and Ethnicity.
        *   Education.
        *   Prevention.
        *   Behavior Modification.

2. Discussion
    a) Needs of the elderly.
    b) How these needs can be met.

3. Recommendations
    Screening and training of employees.
    a) Prevention of elderly abuse, neglect, and maltreatment in institutions and communities.
    b) Identification.
    c) Investigation.
    d) Reporting elderly abuse.

SUMMARY

The specific findings of the study support the hypotheses that:

a) There is an increase in elderly abuse, neglect, and maltreatment.

b) There is a low incidence of reporting elderly abuse, neglect, and maltreatment.

c) The negative attitudes of caregivers have a negative impact on the delivery of care to the elderly.

Both the literature review and the responses to the questionnaire substantiate the findings. For example, Jogerst, Gerald J. et al (2000) indicated that it is estimated that almost four times more new cases of elder abuse, neglect, and maltreatment are substantiated by adult protective services. They mentioned that in 1991, cases of elderly abuse were up to 94 percent from 1986. Family members were said to report 20 percent of the substantiated cases.

Physicians, nurses, and clinics reported only 8.4 percent of the total number of cases. Wolfe (1998) confirmed that over one million Americans who are age 60 or older are victims of abuse in the domestic setting each year. "The full number is not known due to under-reporting. Some experts believe that only 1 in 14 cases is ever reported." George D. Pozgar (1999) wrote that 1 in 8 cases of elderly abuse, neglect, and maltreatment is never reported. Some abusers in institutions were identified as nursing home staff; primary among whom are nurses' aides and orderlies.

Kusmeskus and Tatara (1996) made the following statement, "Sometimes the signs of elder abuse are not recognized and this is responsible for gross under-reporting." They confirmed that in 1996, there were 2.16 million estimated cases reported but the true number could be greater due to under-reporting. One reason they gave could be the fact that many elderly do not leave their homes so that other than family members could see them.

The findings from this study also show that this area requires immediate remediation. The U.S. House Select Committee on Aging (1980) reported that only 1 in 6 cases of elderly abuse is reported.

NEGATIVE ATTITUDE OF ELDERLY CAREGIVERS

The findings of the study also supports the need for better evaluation and interviewing techniques for subsequent employment of prospective elder care workers.

According to Eckley and Vilakazi (1995), "It can also be seen that the educational process for such employees....on a macro level attitudes which result in maltreatment of the elderly can be influenced through increased efforts in community education. Greater awareness and more accurate identification of the problem of elderly victims can lead to the re-shaping of attitudes and broadening of knowledge about abuse and the required services on

43

the micro level, successful preventative knowledge of the phenomenon of the dynamics and the prevention of elderly abuse."

Despite the limitations of the study, and focusing on the findings from questions 8, 9, and 10 of the questionnaire, the researcher advocates further investigation of the healthcare conditions surrounding elderly abuse, neglect, and maltreatment. As further studies may be designed to study and investigate this societal problem, there should be a more systematic approach, involving personal interviews with random samples of elderly caregivers. Further recommendations will be discussed at the end of the chapter. The responses to question 8 of the questionnaire indicate that although training in elderly abuse, neglect, and maltreatment should be mandatory for all employees who provide care for the elderly in that facility, there is a severe deficiency in the compliance rate with training regarding elderly abuse, neglect, and maltreatment.

In responses to question 9, 66 percent of the participants agreed with the question. The answer supports the hypothesis that elderly abuse is on rise. Of the 23 participants, 14 responded that they did not in fact like working with the elderly. In other words only 9 of the participants who responded said they like to work with the elderly. These responses could point to more careful screening of new employees and better training of current employees. It shows that there exists a deficiency in the in-service education system in the long-term care facility that requires that all employees should receive mandatory training in elderly abuse, neglect, and maltreatment. However, the responses to question 8, even though positive, were unexpected, since elderly abuse training is mandatory in the facility where the study was conducted, as well as other elder care institutions in most of the fifty states in the United States of America.

The *New York Daily News* of December 22, 2000 indicated that efforts were being made to reduce the incidence of abuse of the elderly. Dr. Antonio Novella, New York State Health Commissioner, in an article, "We're on Nursing Home Case," wrote the following, "I want to reassure everyone that the respect, dignity, and quality of life for New York's frail and elderly are a top priority for my department, our staff is committed to overseeing all nursing homes to ensure that every resident receives high quality care and we are backing up this commitment to overseeing all nursing homes to ensure that every resident receives high quality care...greater staffing, better training, and more advanced equipment will not totally eliminate deficient nursing home practices...that will take a more informed public and increased responsibility on the part of the nursing home owners to provide a safe environment for their residents and to recruit and retain qualified, compassionate caregivers."

IMPLICATIONS FOR THE DISCIPLINE:

U.S. Healthcare Cost

The number of people over age sixty-five is predicted to double in twenty-five years. As this age group increases, so will the cost of health care, if this trend of elderly abuse is not curtailed. As people age, the risk of developing chronic diseases due to frailty is inevitable. Some of these chronic diseases in question are dementia, diabetes, osteoporosis, and deficiencies in hearing, swallowing, vision, urinary, and gastrointestinal problems. Debilitating complications from some of the chronic conditions such as incontinence, constipation, fractures, confusion, hypo- or hyperglycemia, and chronic pain are situations that are common among the elderly.

The oldest of the old will demand a great proportion of the cost to the United States Health Care Delivery System. The cost greatly increases if the present rate of elderly abuse, neglect, and maltreatment is not only reduced but also totally prevented.

At present, elderly abuse is causing unnecessary spending of U.S. health care dollars. With the proven increase in elderly abuse, health care costs to this end will no doubt also continue to increase.

Culture and Ethnicity

Another important population shift in the United States is the fast growth of ethnic groups; that is a vast increase in the number of elderly people of different ethnic backgrounds and cultures. Some of these individuals do not regard some of the United State's definitions of elderly abuse as wrong doing. For example, Jordan I. Kosberg (1995), in referring to Japanese culture regarding the elderly, stated, "There is a discrepancy between culturally defined normative and actual feelings towards care giving responsibilities." The United States will have to reach a common ground with all the cultures and ethnic groups living in its borders and create a basic standard for determining what constitutes elderly abuse in order to be able to recognize and prevent abuse.

Education

The first step towards prevention is through education both at the community and elderly care institution levels. In the community, education would rest with the Public Health and Social Services authorities to formulate preventive education programs. In elderly care institutions, it would rest with the owners to provide education for their staff. This should be in compliance with state requirements.

At present most states require that all interdisciplinary staff working with the elderly receive training in elder abuse, prevention, identification, and reporting. In many states proven or convicted perpetrators are given strict penalties, up to prison sentences.

As the ethnic groups increase and cultures become more diverse, so will the need for education of elderly care givers from different ethnic backgrounds, to meet the needs of the different ethnic groups. In this way peoples' languages and ethnicity will not be overlooked, misunderstood, or misinterpreted. All elder care facilities should have a language bank to aid in the interpretation of foreign languages. In that way the cries of all elderly for rescue from abuse will be understood.

Prevention: Behavior Modification

Another area of focus in thinking of prevention and care for the elderly is behavior modification. Many elderly people are involved in the following behaviors or habits:

- Drug abuse
- Alcohol abuse
- Gambling
- Smoking
- Poor eating habits

There is clearly a link between elderly abuse, neglect, and maltreatment, and these behaviors and habits from both ends of the spectrum—the victim's end and the abuser's end. These negative behaviors do not only lead to abuse but also lead to poor health. Elderly people, their families, and caregivers who engage in these behaviors should be assisted with education regarding behavior modification. Like children at risk for abuse, the law should remove the elderly from caregivers or family members who are identified to pose a risk of abusing them.

Earlier research revealed that a large percentage of nursing home population have alcohol-related problems. It was also noted that less than 3 percent of the budget of the National Institute on Alcohol Abuse and Alcoholism Research was earmarked for senior citizens. It is believed that alcohol is the drug of choice for many elderly. Reasons identified for alcohol abuse among the elderly are due to situations such as:

- Loneliness
- Widowhood
- Boredom
- Serious illness
- Children leaving home
- Loss
- Depression
- Retirement

These alcohol-related problems are frequently categorized as "behavioral" problems. Elderly people with drug and alcohol problems need to be taught how to cope with problems such as losing family and friends, income, health, and homes on the community level. The Public Health authorities could play an effective role in such ventures.

Care providers who are identified with these behavioral problems should not be allowed to work with the elderly until they are helped to eliminate these behaviors. There are several programs that provide help such as the Alcoholics Anonymous program, drug detoxification, and rehabilitation programs.

DISCUSSION

The literature review and the response to the questionnaire support the hypotheses cited at the beginning of the research. In considering solutions to these problems the following must be brought into focus:

a) The dynamics of aging as outlined by Robert Atchley (1989).
b) The needs of the elderly.

There are certain needs that are specific to the aging person. These needs, when they are not met, impact negatively on the quality of life of the elderly person. It is important for all caregivers to understand those needs. The impact could even be greater to elders who become institutionalized. When some elderly person are institutionalized, they experience many losses including the negative side of Erickson's last milestone that relates to the elderly. Instead of achieving integrity, they sometimes experience despair form their losses. The following are some of the losses they experience:

- Loss of self-esteem
- Loss of self-respect
- Loss of freedom
- Loss of independence
- Loss of family, friends, children, spouse, and home, cherished belongings, and other property
- Loss of privacy
- Loss of love
- Loss of vitality due to increasing physical weakness and other chronic debilitating conditions.
- Loss of control over their lives

HOW THE NEEDS OF THE ELDERLY CAN BE MET

Self Esteem:
The elderly need to feel that they are useful and thought of by others as well.

a) Care givers should help the elderly to reminisce about their past as well as past achievements.

47

b) They need to have their grooming maintained.
c) They need to feel appreciated.
c) They should be allowed to visit and be visited.

Privacy:
Elderly people, especially those who are institutionalized.
a) They need time to be alone.
b) Spouses need time together.
c) Their private concerns should be kept confidential.
d) Knock on their doors before entering.

Loss of Freedom:
Elderly persons should not be made to feel imprisoned or confined. Their sense of freedom should be maintained. For example:
a) They should be allowed freedom of movement as much as is physically possible or can be tolerated. Restraints and side rails should only be used as last resorts to prevent injury to the elderly.
b) The elderly have rights that if violated can result in a feeling of alienation, anger, and depression. For example:
- The right to refuse certain treatment or tests.
- The right to vote.
- The right to choose their own clothing.
- The right to proper nutrition.
- The right to be treated fairly without discrimination.
- The right to an attorney.

Loss of Self Respect:
Elderly people like to feel that others think well of them. For example:
- They should be called by their names
- They should be comforted when they are depressed
- If possible, they should give their permission for someone to touch them and care for them.

Safety:
The elderly should be provided with a safe environment. For example:
- Provide alarms and call-bells for those who are institutionalized.
- Maintain proper environmental temperature.
- Provide proper temperature for meals and for baths.
- There should be proper maintenance of wheelchairs and other devices.
- They should be protected from mis-appropriation of their property by staff and family.

Love for the Elderly:
All elderly persons whether in institutions or at home need to be shown kindness, love, and compassion. For example:
- Show interest in the person.
- Touch them gently when they need to be comforted.
- Maintain confidence and trust by sticking to promise.

All functional abilities related to activities of daily living (ADL's) should be evaluated at the outset in order to establish a baseline and set realistic goals for care and for teaching psychomotor and cognitive skills to elderly persons. Areas of consideration for baseline evaluation are:
- Vision.
- Hearing.
- Tactile sensation.
- Musculoskeletal changes.
- Cognitive functions.
- Mobility.
- Literacy.
- Speech.
- Language.

Attitudes:
Previous research on the relationship between attitudes and behavior suggest that attitudes, cultures, and beliefs towards the elderly greatly influence the care that the elderly receive from caregivers. For example, a caregiver who believes that elderly people are not able to learn new skills, such as toileting or giving him/herself insulin injections, will not try to teach these skills to the elderly individual. This helps to reinforce the stereotype that the elderly are always dependent on others.

RECOMMENDATIONS:
From the literature review and the responses to the questionnaire, several variables or problems were identified. In order to prevent these problems, health care providers who are authorized should follow certain guidelines for the benefit of the elderly. Public Health authorities need to monitor the care of the elderly on the community level.

The following are some important topics to be considered in the prevention of elderly abuse, neglect, and maltreatment in institutions:
- Screening of new employees.
- Training of employees.
- Means of prevention of abuse to institutionalized residents.
- Methods of identifying abuse.
- Methods of investigating abuse.
- Reporting of elderly abuse.

Screening

All prospective employees should have background checks for history of elderly abuse, neglect, and maltreatment, immigration status, criminal involvement, and arrest records. The following are other considerations:

- Employment should be contingent on the furnishing of satisfactory
  references, including proof of education, work, and performance
  history.
- Employees should obtain waivers of written consent regarding
  obtaining the above before employment is offered or before identi-
  fication is issued to the applicant.
- The institution's security department should fingerprint the applicants.
- Information from previous employers regarding the new employees
  should be obtained if the applicants were previously employed.
- Professional licenses and certificates should be validated and verified.
- Applicants should be screened for use of illicit substances by the
  Employees Health Services.
- All information regarding the applicant should be submitted to
  Human Resources Department for the establishment of a file.
- Identification of any risk factor should be grounds for termination
  of the employment or interviewing process.

Training

All employees should be given an orientation period. During this time, the
employee should be monitored for inappropriate behaviors. All elderly care
institutions should provide an ongoing in-service program. Topics such
Elderly Abuse, Neglect, and Maltreatment should be mandatory for members of all disciplines upon employment and on an annual basis. Other abuse
prohibition factors such as the following should be included in the training
or in-service program.

- How to deal with aggressive patients.
- How to deal with catastrophic reactions of patients.
- What constitutes elderly abuse, neglect, and maltreatment?
- How to recognize burn-out, stress, and high levels of frustration in
  caregivers since these could lead to abuse of the patients.
- How and to whom reports of abuse should be made.

Prevention

Upon admission to an elderly care facility, prospective residents and their
families should be provided with information regarding persons to whom
they should report their concerns, incidents, and grievances without fear of
intimidation.

a) Upon admission residents should undergo orientation with regards
   to their rights in the nursing facility. They should also be given

information regarding certain organizations, persons, and telephone numbers for reporting or filing complaints.

b) There should be adequate staff on all shifts to meet the needs of residents.

c) Staff assigned to residents should have adequate knowledge of their required care. The staff should possess the training to be able to provide the necessary care.

d) The staff should be adequately supervised in order to identify inappropriate behaviors such as:

- Rough handling.
- Derogatory language.
- Ignoring call-lights or call-bells.
- Allowing residents who need to go to the bathroom to urinate and defecate in bed.
- Monitoring and assessing of residents' needs and behaviors that might lead to neglect. Such patients include those with history of aggressive behaviors, wandering, those with history of self inflicted injuries, those with communication problems, those who need patience for spoon feeding, and those who are totally dependent upon the staff.

Identification of Abuse

The staff should be trained to identify the following events that could constitute abuse: bruises that are suspicious, complaints of the elderly person, occurrences and their patterns and trends. All employees working with the elderly should be taught the following:

- All accidents and incidents are to be reported to a supervisor.
- An occurrence report must be completed and the resident examined by a doctor.
- The incident report must be submitted to the Director of Nursing, who should determine and coordinate an investigation and if necessary submit a report to State Department. Caregivers in the community should be advised to report falls and other injuries sustained to the elderly person's doctor.

Reporting Elderly Abuse, Neglect, and Maltreatment

Any health care practitioner, patient, or relative can report abuse to the state. In nursing homes, it is the duty of the Director of Nursing or the Administrator to report suspected or proven elderly abuse but any licensed employee can make the report. Reports should be made within twenty-four hours of the occurrence or the next working day. Reporting information should be made available to patients. The office to which reports are made in New York is:

New York State Office, Telephone: (212) 268-6689
A copy of the reporting law should be available from the Institution's Administrator. There is also a twenty-four hour patient care hotline. In New York the number is **toll free (888) 201-4563**
Further information regarding reporting can be obtained by writing to:
New York State
Department of Health
Box 2000
Albany, NY 12220
The employee's supervisor and Director of Nursing determine disciplinary action towards a staff member who is accused of elderly abuse, neglect, or maltreatment. Such discipline could involve suspension, termination, and/or reporting to a professional licensing board and or registry depending on what is proven from the report.

REPORTING GUIDELINES

Charles E Marshall, M.D., et. al. wrote the following article: "Standardized Protocols Designed to Guide the Task of Identifying, Classifying, and Reporting Geriatric Abuse are Evolving," *Geriatrics*, February 2000. The Elder Abuse Prevention Identification and Treatment Act (EAPITA) also contributed to the article. Thus far, no standardized assessment or reporting protocol has gained general acceptance by clinicians.

The article pointed out that many of the proposed reporting protocols are not yet known to health and forensic professionals. It also stated that forty-two of the fifty United States have laws that make reporting of elderly abuse mandatory for health care providers. Elderly abuse reporting is voluntary in other states. New York, North and South Dakota, Pennsylvania, Illinois, Wisconsin, New Jersey, and Colorado are the states that do not require mandatory reporting. Many states protect professionals who make reports through the "Disclosure Confidentiality Laws."

RESOURCES FOR REPORTING ELDER ABUSE

- U.S. Administration on Aging (http://www.aoa.gov)
- National Aging Information Center *(http://www.aoa.dhhs.gov/naic)*
- National Center on aging Abuse *(http://www.gwjapan.com/NCEA)*
- National Citizens Coalition for Nursing Home Reform *(http://www.ncenhr.org)*
- New York Association of Homes and Services for the Aging Tel: (518) 449-2707 *(www.Nyahsa.org)*

Reporting Healthcare Providers Who Abuse the Elderly or Who are Engaged on Other Acts of Professional Misconduct

In 1986, President Reagan signed the Health Care Quality Improvement Act (HCQIA) Title 4 of Public Law 99-660. From this Act, the National Practitioner Data Bank was established on September 1, 1990. The Bank falls under the jurisdiction of the Bureau of Health Professionals within the Department of Health and Human Services. The data bank collects and releases information regarding the professional conduct of health care practitioners such as doctors, nurses, dentists, chiropractors, and other health professionals.

One of the main aims of the data bank is to prevent or restrict incompetent or abusive practitioners from moving from state to state, or from one institution to the next. This is done in an effort to elude discipline or disclosure of their poor or dangerous performance.

Each state has a state board of nursing. In New York State the licensing authority for nurses is:

The State Education Program
Division of Professional Licensing Services
Cultural Education Center
Empire State Plaza
Albany, New York 12230

Information concerning nurses' aides could be obtained by calling:
(1-800-US-SEARCH)

OTHER RECOMMENDATION

- Adequate salaries for workers.
- More surveillance cameras in elder care facilities.
- More unannounced state inspections and other government intervention into reports of elderly abuse.
- More social workers for elder home visits in the community.
- Mandatory education programs regarding the needs of the elderly, the dynamics of aging, and abuse prevention.
- More structured interviews and stricter investigation of prospective workers for the elderly.
- Stricter laws regarding reporting of elderly abuse, neglect, and maltreatment.
- More assisted living homes for those elderly who do not need the confinement of nursing homes.
- More trained state inspectors for nursing homes and other elder care facilities.
- Continuous Quality Improvement programs in all eldercare institutions.

CONCLUSION OF CHAPTER 5

This chapter concludes the study by discussing the summary of the study, discussion of the problem, and recommendation for preventing and dealing with the problem of the Elderly Abuse, Neglect, and Maltreatment. Further investigation of the topic is expected as the aging population increases and cultures and ethnicity become more diverse. The topic appears to be one of concern to many nations of the world. Prevention of the problem begins with compassion and understanding of caregivers both in private homes and institutions.

BIBLIOGRAPHY

Atchley, Robert C. " Continuity Theory of Normal Aging" *The Gerontology Society* Vol. 29. No 2.1989

Amou Alike and Zambito T., " Nursing Home Deaths Soar." *New York Daily News*, February 15, 2001

Bowers, Joan E. " Caring for the Elderly," *Nursing 98*, 1998

Bezon, Joan "Approaching Drug Regimens with a Therapeutic Dose Of Suspicion." *Geriatric Nursing*.July/August 1991.

Butler Robert N., et. al.:" Aging and Mental Health Prevention of Caregiver Overload Abuse and Neglect.:" *Geriatric Magazine*, July 1992

Calderone, J. and Zambito, T. "Medicaid Fat Cats: Owners Make Millions Off Private Nursing Homes." *New York Daily News*, July 31, 2000

"Nursing Home Abuse Allegations on Rise." *New York Daily News*, August 2,2000

"DA Says Nurse Withheld Patients' Drugs." *New York Daily News*, August 14, 2000

"Nursing Home Abuse Allegations on Rise." *New York Daily News*, September/2000

"New York Hit on Nursing Homes: State Inspectors Missed Violations." *New York Daily News*, October 2000

"5 L.I. Nurses Charges Cover-up of Patient Abuse." *New York Daily News*, November 7, 2000

"Senior Care Nightmare." *New York Daily News*, November 2000

"Cover-up Abuse Case Focus." *New York Daily News*, November, 2000

"Feeling No Pain: Nursing Home Raking It In." *New York Daily News*, January 12, 2001

Deets, Horace B. "The Older Americans' Act:A Crowning Achievement." *AARP Bulletin*, December 2000

Duka Walt, "OAA (Older Americans' Act): A Major Exception—Key Bill:" *AARP Bulletin*, December 2000.

Fromhart, Stephen G. "Are Alzheimer's Special Care Units Effective?" *Long Term Care*. Rehabilitation. May, 1995

Holder, Elma L. "Deemed Status For Inspections Does Not Serve Public Interest." *McKnights Long Term Care*. October 1, 2000

Jogerst, Gerald J. et al. "Community Characteristics Associated with Elder Abuse." *Journal of the American Geriatric Society*. 2000

Jonas, Steven and Kovner, Anthony R. "Health Care Delivery In the United States: Aging and Ethnic Changes In the Population." Spring 1998. *J.A.M.A. Journal of the American Medical Association*.

Johnson, Beverly. " Older Adults Suggestion For Health Care Providers Regarding Discussion of Sex." *Geriatric Nursing* March/April 1997

Keller, Suzanne and Light, Donald Jr. "Participant Observation," *Sociology*, Second Edition, pg 46. Alfred N Knopf. NY,1979

Kosberg, Jordan I. and Garcia, Juanita L. *Elder Abuse: International and Cross-Cultural Perspectives*. The Hawthorn Press Inc. 1995

Kuzmeskus, Lisa and Toshio Tatara. "Types of Elder Abuse in Domestic Settings." *National Center on Elder Abuse Bulletin*. March 1999.

Morris, Robin. "Elder Abuse: What the Law Requires." *RN Magazine*, August 1998

Marshall Charles, E. "Standardized Protocols Designed to Guide the Task of Identifying, Classifying, and Reporting Geriatrics Abuse Are Evolving." *Geriatrics Magazine*, February 2000.

Nores, Taula Hannele. "What Is Most Important for Elders in Institutional Care in Finland." *Geriatrics Magazine*. March/April 1997

Novello, Antonio C. "Commish Responds; We're on Nursing Home Case." *New York Daily News*, December 22, 2000

Plummer, Helen, RN." Domestic Violence and Abuse of the Elderly, Advance." *Nurses Magazine*. June 11, 2001, Vol.1, No.1

Sampter Jeanne and Voss Barbara J. "Challenging the Myths of Aging." *Geriatric Nursing*. January/February 1992

Sauto-Novak, Debra A. "Seven Keys To Assessing the Elderly." *Nursing 88*. August 1988.

Smith, Margaret K and Sullivan, Jean M. Nurses' and Patients' Perception of Most Important Caring Behaviors." *Long Term Care Magazine*. March/April, 1997

Appendix I

Questionnaire

Your cooperation in completing this questionnaire and returning it in one week will be greatly appreciated. It is not necessary to include your name. All answers will be kept confidential. Please circle "A" <u>Yes</u>, "B" <u>No</u>, or "C" <u>Undecided</u>.

1. Have you ever thought of becoming old? A, B, C
2. Is your mother alive? A, B, C
3. Is your father alive? A, B, C
4. Did you grow up with your parents? A, B, C
5. Are any of your parents or grandparents over age 65? A, B, C
6. Is there an elderly person living in your home? A, B, C
7. Do you like working with elderly patients? A, B, C
8. Have you had training regarding elderly abuse, neglect, and maltreatment? A, B, C
9. Do you feel that abuse of the elderly in Nursing Homes is increasing? A, B, C
10. If you witness or suspect abuse of an elderly person would you report it? A, B, C

Appendix II
Graphical Representations of
Responses to Questions 1-10

Reponse to Question 1

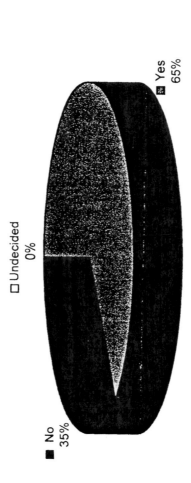

No
35%

Undecided
0%

Yes
65%

Legend:
Yes
No
Undecided

A greater percentage of participants have concerns about growing old.

Response to Question 2

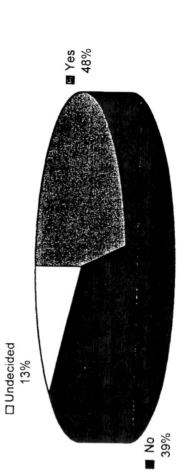

Approximately 15 of the participants' mothers are alive.

Response to Question 3

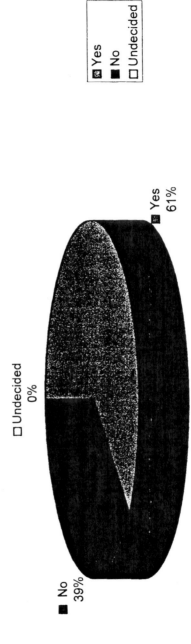

Yes
61%

No
39%

□ Undecided
0%

☒ Yes
■ No
□ Undecided

A larger percentage of participants have a relationship with an older family member.

Answer to Question 4

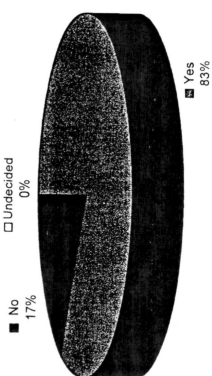

□ Undecided
0%

■ No
17%

▨ Yes
83%

A greater percentage experience parent/child bonding.

▨ Yes
■ No
□ Undecided

Answer to Question 5

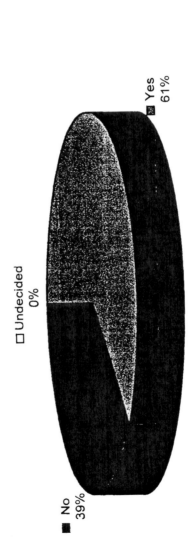

Undecided
0%

No
39%

Yes
61%

Most people have parents and grandparents over 65.

Yes
No
Undecided

Answer to Question 6

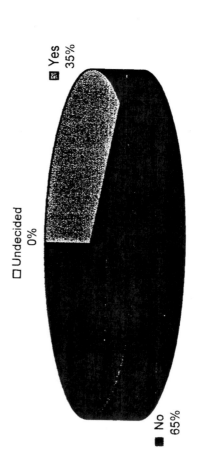

Undecided
0%

No
65%

Yes
35%

- Yes
- No
- Undecided

A smaller percentage of participants have a relationship with an elderly person.

Answer to Question 7

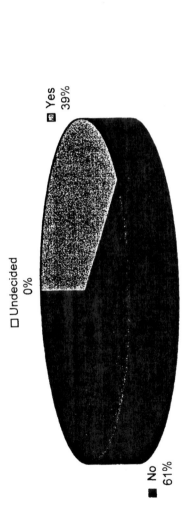

Undecided 0%

No 61%

Yes 39%

Yes
No
Undecided

Most individuals do not enjoy working with the elderly.

Answer to Question 8

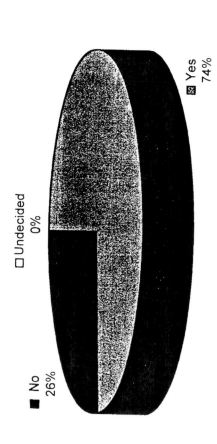

Undecided
0%

No
26%

Yes
74%

- Yes
- No
- Undecided

A greater percentage had training in the care of the elderly.

Answer to Question 9

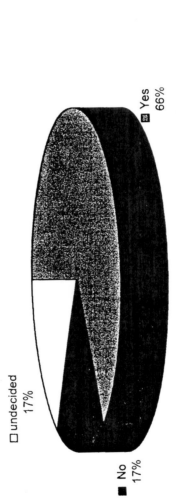

Yes 66%

No 17%

undecided 17%

Yes
No
undecided

Most individuals felt that there was abuse of the elderly.

Answer to Question 10

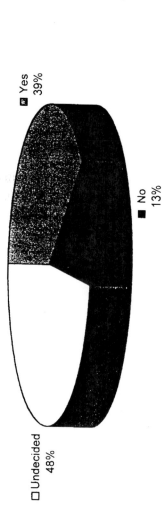

Yes
39%

No
13%

Undecided
48%

- Yes
- No
- Undecided

The majority of the participants were undecided about reporting incidents of elderly abuse.